Cursory of Emotions

Collection of short stories

Dr. Bhagyesh Cheta

ISBN 978-93-5610-128-9
© Dr. Bhagyesh Cheta 2022
Published in India 2022 by Pencil

A brand of

One Point Six Technologies Pvt. Ltd.
123, Building J2, Shram Seva Premises,
Wadala Truck Terminal, Wadala (E)
Mumbai 400037, Maharashtra, INDIA
E connect@thepencilapp.com
W www.thepencilapp.com

Author biography

He has completed his bachelor's in dental surgery from GDCH, Ahmedabad and is currently pursuing masters in endodontic from same college

CONTENTS

Introduction

This book is collection of short stories I had written during pandemic revolving around various kind of human emotions

Stories of life

1. Silent Wonder

Sometimes we feel life is miserable and God has been unfair to us Rishi was going through rough phase of his life continuous quarell of his parents, being bullied by classmates ,poor academic performance all made him depressed if this was not enough one day he missed his school bus but he managed to catch an autorickshaw "Are you getting late for school " rishi turned his head towards this calm and poised voice of a boy sitting next to him nodding yes He rushed to his class room with fear of getting punished During break he saw the same boy in the ground next to his school giving instructions to other fellows. For few days these continued "Are you preparing something" Rishi asked the boy, he replied yes In which grade are you studying rishi asked further, the boy replied in composed voice 8th grade he added we are preparing a skit for charity event for cancer patients "Great" Rishi replied Are you living nearby "Balshanskar Orphanage " boy replied with gentle smile on his face I am suffering from multiple myeloma the boy added Rishi asked with shock then why don't you take rest "When I was diagnosed with multiple myeloma I was bedridden completely shattered as if my life has ended I became so weak was not able to even stand I knew I m going to die but I realized this the life it's his job to place hurdles in our way and it's our job to cross it and move ahead" "Then how did you managed your self "Rishi asked. "I started motivating myself we all knew that we have sense in our selves to cop up with situation and to see the life the way we wish All of us have inbuilt strength to deal with situation and cross the hurdles of life it's just that we have to identify it and follow" the boy replied Rishi was having blast of emotions in his head as he thought with life being harsh to the boy how sportingly he is managing while I m having such a great life and still I complain about it

******

2. Passion Never Dies

She continued her writing without giving second thought about her current situation mother of ten month old baby, getting divorce from husband, recent death of her mother.

She was able to manage all these situation as she was doing her job as a literature teacher at nearby school but her life needs her to give more test as she lost her job now the condition became so worst that it was even difficult for her to find shelter and feed her baby and that too single handedly.

Above all these she has to complete her book, she was able to find new job and temporary shelter but now none of the publisher were ready to publish her book but like her life problems she didn't gave up here also

Finally she got her book published with early slower response it picked up pace later on by time passing she became billionaire author and once in an interview when she was asked did you ever felt you should stop writing she replied "Never, I knew writing is my passion and passion never dies"

******

3. One Last time

The phone ranged with WhatsApp message reading "Plz gather near the lecture hall as we are going to click last group photo" how emotional that moment was, we all came to college as unknown individuals became friends made so much memories spent most precious 5 years of our life got degree and now Once again we will be on separate paths

This was the last day of our college life after 4 years of study and 1 year of internship today we are just going to end our memorable journey We all were cherishing those priceless moments which will now be memories forever Some of them were clicking photos some of them were crying but every one was together that feeling which cannot be expressed in words With heavy heart CR of our class called everyone shared some beautiful lines and asked us to stand accordingly as we are going to click last group photo

With the end of photo session now it was the time to bid goodbye to each other but everyone was cheering laughing hugging crying like literally the roller coaster of emotions were there as deep down each of us wanted to relive the moment for ONE LAST TIME

****

4. Jeet ki Asha

They both were toppers of their class and both used to be good friend beside being always ready to give competition to each other friends used to tease them in school by each others name but they hardly used to pay any attention to it Now both were waiting for their board results and to everybody's surprise she choose arts even after securing Rank 1 in state and he choose science being 2 in state

He got admission in IIT and she went to JNU to study philosophy even after receiving thousands of advice regarding better career options because she knew her interest, but they always remain in contact with each other

With time they discover how much they love each other but their first preference was their career After settling in their respective jobs and with family's permission finally they got married that too in simple manner After 2 years of the marriage Jeet(he) received his dream job offer from US but Asha(she) always want to serve her nation So as they had already decided to put their career first both decided to pursue their dreams as they always used to respect each others decision

Whenever someone asked them "Then what's the meaning of marriage if you live separately" They used to answer "Marriage is not about just staying together it's about respecting each other's thoughts"

******

5. Glass half Empty

A psychologist walked around a room while teaching stress management to an audience. As she raised a glass of water, everyone expected they'd be asked the 'half empty or half full' question. Instead, with a smile on her face, she inquired . . . 'How heavy is this glass of water?'

Answers called out ranged from 250 grams to 500 grams.

She replied . . . 'The absolute weight doesn't matter. It depends on how long I hold it. If I hold it for a minute, it's not a problem. If I hold it for an hour, I'll have an ache in my arm. If I hold it for a day, my arm will feel numb and paralyzed. In each case, the weight of the glass doesn't change, but the longer I hold it, the heavier it becomes.'

She continued . . . 'The stresses and worries in life are like that glass of water. Think about them for a while and nothing happens. Think about them a bit longer and they begin to hurt. And if you think about them all day long, you will feel paralyzed - incapable of doing anything.'

It's important to remember to let go of your stresses. As early in the evening as you can, put all your burdens down. Don't carry them through the evening and into the night.

Remember to put the glass down!

****

6. Angels in Heaven Now

What we wished we did leaving no regrets behind its just we didn't ever thought of death like this we always wanted to cure others ailments as it was our duty and we did

We never wanted to face such helpless condition but we fought as much as we can even at cost of our lives without thinking about our family who like all other wanted us to stay at home safely

But how can we withdraw ourselves from such situation when everyone around us was suffering We had seen so many births but we never wanted to see so many deaths like literally that much leaving no space for burial

Who would have thought that the thing which we are curing will be the cause of our death As now we are free from all these residing in heaven we just wish the way we died no one should die like that

******

7. Life and Death

All our life is journey between birth and death

As we celebrate birthdays every year to reminisce the birth , the years old concept of celebrating death is still alive and the place well known for this is VARANASI according to mythology it's the best place to die and achieve moksha (the ultimate peace)

The famous death hotel known as MUKTI BHAWAN situated on the bank of holy river Ganga in Varanasi is famous across globe for giving accommodation to the dying ones to fulfill their wish of attaining salvation in this holy town that too free of cost

Presently this place is run by Dalmia group and people can stay here for 15 days as you have to die within these period Those who had intuitions of death mainly resides here where after their death every rituals are performed by the priest residing there

It's not just that nowadays it has became one of the famous tourist spot in Varanasi as people used to visit this place just to witness the condition and feelings of those on deathbeds.

****

8. Memories

Old man waiting for his turn outside the hospital OPD was scrolling his phone. There were no new messages, no missed calls. He smiled wryly and remembered the times when his phone used to ring continuously with messages and calls. How he could never imagine a moment with the phone. But now it almost never rang. May be the world had forgotten him or may be the world that he knew as world no longer existed.

He opened the photo collection on his phone and started scrolling through the time stamped pictures from last so many years. Some of them looked totally unfamiliar and He wondered where and why did he ever click them. He saw some beautiful places and wished to be there again. He tried to remember why and where he had taken each picture. Location and dates were of great help. He saw smiles, he saw family, he saw friends. He felt emotions coming back to him with each picture.

That day he understood the importance of those moments and understood why camera was invented, why our phones have cameras. We all have that desire to capture and freeze the good times somehow so that we have a mechanism to somehow recreate the feelings at a later date, long after those times are over and those people are gone.

And then he raised his phone, posed for the camera to click a selfie at the hospital. This was another precious moment worth capturing because he was still alive.

People around him looked at him with disbelief and contempt and whispered, oldie is behaving like a school kid

****

9. Farewell

Pankaj was bit sad and excited also as it was the last day of his job as he was getting retired after serving for 30 years it was like second home to him but now he would miss all these things and have to begin a new life

The farewell party was organised by the company as he was one of the reputated personality but all these celebrations made nostalgic and he thought how every end adds value to journey right from school days where he had studied from nursery to 12th in a single school so he had so many memories and finally when it all ended with farewell it made all special

Then again with college the same thing happened and with farewell all those moments ended and now this

He thought how everything in the beginning looks boring and exhausting but as gradually we lead towards the end it becomes enjoyable and we become more attached towards it

That's why actually the farewell is celebrated so that we can enjoy the end making it also memorable and plan a new beginning

****

10. Insomnia

Mayank became restless as he was not able to sleep even after trying several things to induce sleep he failed Now due to this he developed severe headache and he started feeling weakness even during daytime he tried to fall asleep but all went into vain Now he concerned the psychologist and he took his detailed history which stated that earlier he used to sleep regularly between 11 to 11:30 pm but after these from few days when all these quarantine happened he used to watch series upto 2 to 3 am gradually he became addicted and now he used to watch till morning 5 as he thought it's common because he knew many people do the same

The doctor explained him that because of this his sleep wake rhythm which regulated by pineal gland is disrupted so because of its abnormal function he might feel sleepy during day time and even the whole day would become tiring He concluded that Mayank was suffering from Insomnia which is mild in nature and in early stage but if it's not cured it might progress to higher stage

 So he prescribed him some sedative and asked him to strictly follow his instructions not to watch anything for more than 2 hrs consecutively relax the eyes by closing it for 5 minutes at every 1 or 2 hrs and go to sleep by 11 pm He further told that this has become common problem nowadays as people are so much addicted to their phones that they don't even realize that their eyes and brain also want some relaxation and end up with insomnia and other severe psychiatric disorders even some them had developed severe eyesight problems but still most of them are taking it lightly Now it's high time to realise until it becomes too late to understand

****

11. The last wish

The prisoner was about to be hanged but before that the jailer asked his last wish he smiled with tears in his eyes and replied I just want to die seeing my mother's photo and please make sure that after my death this she receive this letter then he offered last prayer and his mother's photo was kept in front of him and lever was pulled

Later when jailer read the letter he got tear in his eyes as it was written "Mother, I might be the worst son on the earth but you are the best mom Never curse your upbringing and never feel guilty about it as you always tried your level best to make sure we get all happiness In this life I could not give you anything except pain and suffering but I wish if there is anything like re birth I would be your son and I would make sure to give you all the happiness in the world By the time you will receive this letter I won't be there but please live your life happily as I would be more happier watching you from above"

12. Struggles

"Struggles make men more stronger "

We have so many examples of people after facing so much hardships finally achieves skyscraper success and one such story is of Charlie Chaplin

He was so poor that his mother developed psychosis due to syphilis and malnutrition and was sent to mental asylum his father got separate immediately after his birth and he used to stay with his mother he was sent to work even before he was 9 .

After his mother's condition he used to stay with his father but he was so alcoholic that he hardly used to pay any attention towards him so Chaplin worked at various places to survive later his father died of cirrhosis and his mother condition also became worse

Amid all these he used to work at theatre in plays which he loved to do but it took time for people to recognise his talent Gradually his plays became so popular that he was offered movies but initially his movies didn't worked so he returned to theatre but then he decided to write act direct the movie himself and the rest we all know how much People loves him today also

Despite going lot of suffering in life he always ensure to entertain people that made him such an extraordinary personality to be remembered forever

13. Those were the Days

Those were the days when every student used to eagerly wait for summer vacation and after all exhaustions of exams and year long studies they finally can now enjoy in their own way those were days when there were no android phones and for all children and teens the actual enjoyment was playing super Mario , contra , ninja and thousands of other video games by inserting that green chip those were days when mornings used to start with outdoor games afternoon with indoor games and night with games like hide and seek , ice pise and lot more games which had now become extinct those were days where citylights used to visit village and their hometown to enjoy summer vacation during those days there used to be vcds and DVDs where people used to watch movie with CDs and for all mango lovers those days are like their year long awaited days keeping aside the chaos of result announcement those were days where people used to await a lot to watch even their board results as internet was not that much common but still the enjoyment was full those carefree summer days where each day of vacation has its own value and its own story to tell

14. Because, I love you

Saumya and Sachin were classmates and as they used to live nearby they used to go in same school van they were normal friends and used to share Tiffin but as they grow up they fall in love with late night studies during board to spending time together and going on trip in vacation they loved each others company so much that even their friends realized that how much they love eachother they even choose same college and stream now everyone around them including their family was aware of their love but they advised them to first focus on studies as they have rest of their life to look for eachother but they were could hardly resist and as soon as they complete their graduation they convinced their family for engagement

Now they started looking out for job but Sachin ended up joining his father's business while Saumya started dancing class she always used to do so even after being busy in their lives they used to spend so much with eachother Everyone used to call them as perfect lovebirds One day Saumya was going for her dance class and she met with accident Sachin rushed to the hospital but doctor told them that it was too late and Saumya has died due to acute blood loss

What Saumya can't go like that leaving me alone till date Sachin can't believe that she is not alive he used to talk with her every day he still believe that she is around him his family had tried a lot and he also went under psychological counseling but nothing can change his belief everyday he used to write about the time they had spent together For people this was madness but for him it was his love

15. Path for others

There are lots of stories around us to inspire us and it can definitely change our perspective towards life one such lesson which I learnt is about a boy who thought to bring a change so that what he experienced no one else can

His father left him and his mother alone so for him to continue his study became difficult because after all education in recent times is all about money but he decided to change his field of interest but with that he came up with idea of founding an NGO for those like him who want to pursue their dreams but can't do due to lack of financial resources though he himself was having economical crisis

But once he decided to start he knew that there will be many hurdles in his path but just by thinking he can't let it go and today also he has to work hard to convince people to fund him but now he had made this his dream so that he enjoys chasing it

16. Perception

We all had studied enough about equality but does it exists in real life No

It is always seen that the more powerful person try to curb those who are weaker than them as if there power will be with them forever

Dominating other people with position has been part of life since long time In today's world Power and Fame are two important that can easily influence the people

Every human in this world try to prove themselves better than other and in this rat race they don't care about anyone's emotions but why why we have to prove ourselves stronger than other Can't we be what we are and who are these people making decisions about us and what makes you stronger or weaker

It's our mind and our thoughts that are making this distinction and we are letting others to influence us It's just we have to change our perception to judge anyone

17. Criticism

Criticism is inborn talent of every human and it's also the occupation of some mankind

We don't want to enter into debate about whether criticism is good or bad because it's actually the view point of people and it's okay until it is stretched too much

If someone donates money for any education purpose then also people criticize by saying what's the big deal he is having so much money that it won't matter him even if he donates it

So at every phase of life it's obvious for anyone to face criticism and to some extent it's good also so that the person can improve his skills but if it becomes too much then it can ruin the life also as it is said that everything must be in balance

There are lots of example of people who have faced lots of criticism and had become popular without it affecting them

on the other side there are many more examples of those who had destroyed that life just because of criticism

So basically it's upto us how we handle it and to what extent it impacts us

18. Mindset

Thoughts are the strongest weapons of mankind as they have ability to change life

The positive thoughts can make us cross all the barriers to achieve success

Most of our actions are actually the reciprocation of our thoughts and beliefs with stronger mindset we can even defeat the biggest enemy even the world around us is also influenced by our thoughts

The famous celebrities of all time have mentioned in their interviews that it's actually the affirmation that had paved their way to success

Oprah Winfrey being born in poor family always believed that once she would be billionaire and that mindset helped her at each moment to move ahead because we all are bound by our thinking and sometimes it prohibit ourselves from achieving big it just we have to be affirmative

19. Precognition

Sometimes what we say just casually becomes true and sometimes the events happen exactly what we had dreamt unknowingly

The boy was ready to celebrate his birthday with his family at the exotic location in foreign country but before he was leaving for that he hugged his friends and became emotional his friends were surprised with this and asked why he was behaving like this he laughed and said this might be last time I am seeing you I might die then he said oh come on I was just making fun don't worry I will be fine

But he was unknown with the fact that what his destiny would have decided and his flight crashed causing death of 56 passengers including him

Precognition, which is presense of the things going to happen it's actually seen in all human like all other senses but it's still debatable that it is actually the science or just causality Still no evidence has been found that specific part of brain is responsible for this and how it occurs but there such cases happening in our life which can make us believe in this

20. Feeling of freedom

Now just two more months we will be here and after that we ..... These were the words of the prisoner who was serving tea to us as we were doing the health camp for them

It was for first time we were interacting with prisoner as much was heard about how dangerous they are and we should not trust them but what we experienced was totally different although they were the exceptions but still when you actually listen to their you get emotional and one such story was of bavu

He and his wife were jailed since past 13 years in charge of murder of two people he said that when they were found guilty their child was of 2 years as both his parents were in jail he was raised by his grandfather but after few years he also died and then he went with his uncle but then he incured loss in business so he was not able to take care of my son so he was sent to helphouse where such left alone children lives however he used to visit us regularly so we could see his face with watery eyes he said now he is preparing for his board exams and finally we will be with him

He added that we always used to regret that if we were able to control our anger we would have given a better future to our son and would have seen him growing up

21. Chivalry

Chivalry is what every boy should be taught nowadays from childhood because the kind of society we are heading towards is not at all good and the mindset of every human is best developed from his early age and influenced by his surroundings

What a man will see he will follow the same so first of all every parents should learn to mould his child thought as nowadays even the young child are indulged in such a crime that are beyond our imagination and what all is responsible for this is their mindset recently the boys locker room issue is making headlines and from where such dirt arises its all from surrounding and thoughts

Nowadays every wants their child to be best and everyone want to live in high standard but they fail to reach basic morals of life and in some cases even parents are not having such sense So ultimately all these will result in development of society of criminals

Like we teach how to walk talk eat all such basic things similarly every boy should be taught how to respect a girl So that we can build a healthy society where we don't have to fight for gender equality

22. Rare Fighter

Very rarely we came across such fighters and sharing story of one such fighter battling rarest disease on earth in her own words

About 6 years ago, my life changed forever. At the age of 19 I was diagnosed with a rare brain disease called Moyamoya. In Japanese this means "puff of smoke." My carotid arteries were formed narrow, causing very little blood going to my brain & if you saw an MRI of it, it literally looked like a puff of smoke. Majority of my life up to that point I was pretty asymptomatic and wouldn't think twice about something being wrong. I would be on airplanes and look like a zombie to all those around me. I went up in the mountains in Switzerland, and instead of enjoying a beautiful view and an epic snowball fight, I was yet again, a zombie. The high altitudes we're making it more difficult for my brain to get any blood, putting me at extreme risk for a stroke. Fortunately, in March of 2014, after a beautiful day spent with my mom, I suffered from a Transient Ischemic Attack, aka, a mini stroke. I had realized I had multiples of these leading up to that day, however, due to ignorance, I did not pay much attention to them. That day, after spending countless hours in the emergency room with more doctors that I can count on my hand, and more tests that I could imagine, I finally got my diagnosis. If I said I didn't think my world shattered and I didn't sob my heart out, I would be lying. After a whole bunch of tests and consults, the reality of the situation was that either I get brain surgeries or I die. The thought of having my brain cut into & prodded at was the most terrifying thing I ever had to think of. Thankfully, with the support and love from my family & friends and the amazing neurosurgeon I had, I was able to go through two successful major brain surgeries without any long term complications. Even though it took me extra time to finish school, I'm thankful to be alive. I was able to graduate, pass my boards, and work as a licensed physical therapist with a new attitude & appreciation for life!

23. A moment of Gasp

It was my biology paper of 12th board I was confident enough about the exam and I was thorough with the subject , the timings of the paper was of afternoon so after having lunch I packed my bag and me and my mom got ready

After waiting for 15 minutes we finally got auto though my exam centre was hardly 15 minutes away from my home but my mom always used to tell that it's better we reach the centre early as we don't know anything can happen in journey So we reached the centre and still half and hour was there for exam to start

Everybody was carrying books with them and I can see many of them were tensed my friend called me and I went to him and he informed me that seating arrangement for today's exam is changed so go and check your class number it's mentioned there on notice board I opened my bag and searched for receipt and I was completely shocked as my compass in which I used to carry receipt was not there My mom asked me and she told me relax don't panic I will be back quickly even my friends consoled me but all negative thoughts were coming to my mind I was so much worried that I started shivering

The bell rang for entry of students everyone started moving in and I was still waiting for my mom I even told to the gate keeper but he said we can't allow you Now almost everyone was gone inside I was standing outside totally nervous But suddenly an autorickshaw came and my mom called me and gave the receipt in my hand and I literally started running Luckily I entered the class on time and my exam went really well and I scored 97/100.

24. She is happy, Now

She always used to ask me what's there in this WhatsApp that everybody used to spend hours and hours on that when WhatsApp was new in the market

Finally when she got the android phone that one of mine as I purchased new one she used to tell everyone that she is on WhatsApp now I used to get annoyed and tell her that Mom it's common nowadays and everyone has it but for her it was the total new experience and she was so much willing to use it that every day she used to ask me please add these number and that

Initially she was so much indulged in it that every now and then she used to ask me how to use Sometimes I felt like I should not have made her profile but she was so curious about it that she used to ask every single thing

Slowly she started learning by herself and everytime she was added in new group she used to tell us about that and we were never interested in it She used to read all messages and then used to share with us So Sometimes I used to say please mom we don't want to listen please don't irritate us

But we never knew that it was just enjoyment for her She used to say that sparing sometime on this used give her break from all those monotonous stuff

25. Artwork of Life

""One incident can change your entire life and just before you plan anything life makes a new plan and puts before you

Years ago I was preparing for my school exams and it was march so you can see everywhere people used to talk about studies and exams however I was happy go lucky person but I used to study at my own time and used to score good but I was so much into the art that I used to make Paintings portraits and lot other it was like my hands were more comfortable with paint brush than pens and I was sure to pursue career in it

But my destiny had another plans for me I was returning to my home from tutions and a car just came hit my cycle from behind I lost my balance and fell down before I could even understand anything the driver rushed the car over my hand and then next thing I remember was that I was in hospital

When I was out of ICU I couldn't even believe I had lost my hand and now what next I will be doing in my life

It not just made me physically handicapped but also mentally. Everyone around me try their best to bost me up but I knew I will never be that again now it was just the matter of survival without any goals but after lot of counseling I regain my confidence and started believing that I still have one hand to create wonders ""

And that's how I managed to be in front of you all receiving this prestigious art award

26. Holy Soul

All along her life she had been adjusting so that all other feel comfortable regardless of her own contentment Right from parents husband and children's she lived her life in accordance to them Why because she thought that's how life works She had such kind of nature that she used to easily blend with the person she meets

She was not that much cash rich but she was rich by heart She always insisted that not to perform any ritual after her death as she doesn't want to bother anyone and likewise her death was also of similar kind (sudden heart attack) without giving trouble to anyone and still we weep cherishing the journey of that holy soul

27. Scary Chills

"Don't go by staircase Use lift" Watchman instructed us as we were in hurry to attend our classes at 4th floor we waited for the lift but it was at 9th floor so without wasting time we decided to climb the stairs

At around 10 pm our classes got finished but as I and my 2 friends were having doubts so we stayed there to solve it after completing we went down in the lift but suddenly it stopped at 3rd floor we thought someone might be waiting for it but there was no one and even all the shops on that floor were closed we pressed the button but the doors didn't closed So we decided to go by staircase

On reaching second floor I heard someone whispering we followed the voice and walked towards the shop but it was already closed then suddenly we hear knock at doors of that closed shop Now we knew that something is wrong here so without thinking further we started running towards the staircase but we felt like some one is holding our legs tightly it was difficult for us to even step forward so we started shouting for help but no was there on that floor We took out our cell phones but it was all vein as there was no network

We were totally blank as it was our worst nightmare coming true now we had no clue about how to escape from this situation..

As it was already 1030pm all the shops were closed We were completely helpless again we heard the noise asking for help we were extremely frightened as we were not able to walk but somehow I managed to crawl and I heard someone climbing stairs on first floor so I shouted for help but no one responded then suddenly my friend shouted "see the lift is working" I tried to stand up and walk but failed as I felt like someone has tied my legs tightly I told my friends we have to reach towards the lift anyhow we literally crawled towards the lift and I don't know from where so much energy came inside us we managed to get inside it as soon as we entered the lift we were able to walk we felt like someone has literally released our feet we reached ground floor one of my friend started crying seeing this the Watchman came and asked what happened we told him the entire incident and how we managed to escape He said that this has happened to many people as the second floor of the building is haunted there was one maid who committed suicide in one of the shop of second floor after that it is believed that her ghost used to haunt that floor whoever purchased the shop at second floor have to close it either because of loss or some other reason Many of them had seen the lady in black attire at second floor Even I had experienced paranormal activity so I used to warn everyone at night to avoid going there but you are lucky that you managed to escape as it is said where there is evil there is good also that helped you

28. Sigh of relief

It was 5 pm the wind speed started rising we were constantly watching news everyone was locked in their houses and continuously enchanting prayers, the hustling sounds produced by the wind was increasing every minute we closed all the doors and windows as instructions were already given by the government officials and the landfall process had already started

With every passing minutes our heartbeat was going up as the wind speed was increasing and after few minutes all the network was gone we can't watch TV neither we can connect with anyone on phones but this was just the beginning as the real wrath was going to take place next at around 6:30 pm the electricity supply went off and the sound of wind became so high that we can't hear any other thing my parents and grandmother were sitting in the drawing room and I was seating next to window trying to see outside but then a loud noise came and we could sense it was from our house we went into my room and what we saw that my entire room was messed up and strong wind was not even allowing us to fix the window which was broken by strong blow of wind

The speed was such high that we felt that we might be carried away now the things became so worst as there was no electricity no network we were completely cut off from outer world and the rain and breeze was making difficult even to see outside my grandmother started crying as she said that she had never witnessed such situation in her entire life we all were scared as the cyclone was approaching the things were becoming much worse at one point of time we felt that our building is shaking and now we all are going to die we were constantly doing prayers and suddenly another loud noise came and before we can sense anything doors started banging even though they were closed the rain water was coming from my room and then our entire house was flooded but we were just praying for everything to be fine then after an hour the electricity came and what we can see is that our entire house was really messed up but now the wind speed started going down and we felt a sigh of relief

29. Wings to fly

Chandni had all those luxuries which every teenager dream about but what everyone can't see was behind that all what miseries she was facing she had number of maids to take care of her but not the parents who always used to remain busy in their own world

She had so many friend but not a single closed one to share her pains and pleasure She had so much to tell and all these used to make her frustrated all the time She had all restrictions as they were much reputated and these used to make her feel uncomfortable as she always want to enjoy and live the small moment of her life

She knew every concern her family was showing to her was superficial and they don't even bother or care about her emotions as they took interest in what she was doing in school and her interest She knew as long as she was with her family she will not enjoy the life so she strongly insisted of getting into the boarding away from her town so she can live carefree life in her own terms Finally her parents agreed and then she finally set herself free as if the birds are allowed to fly after long caging

30. Chasing Mussoorie

Manoj's mom got angry on him as he again went for sleep despite getting late for coaching as it was routine for him to dream about the LBSNAA the place where every civil servant is trained as Manoj was preparing for the UPSC exams

That year he was not able to clear the prelims also but he consoled himself by saying that it was just his first try but next year again he failed and now he started feeling the pressure as all his friends had started earning and they were having jobs while his future was uncertain and above all his neighbours and relatives were always used to ask how many times he will try but he still kept hopes high and in third try he cleared both prelims and mains now he felt some sigh of relief but interview was still left

Unfortunately just a week before his interview his father had cardiac arrest and he passed away but he gave the interview and he missed the cut off again Now he got depressed as all responsibilities were on his head now and he became frustrated and started searching for jobs Though he didn't get the one which he wanted but he thought something is better than nothing

After the routine 9 to 6 job he used to get tired and found very difficult to study Slowly his priorities started shifting and now his goal was to earn more money for his family so he started doing night shifts also, this continued for months and again the forms for UPSC exams were out he filled the form but he hardly used to get time to study he gave the prelim and cleared it but then again he was left with two options either to leave the job or to forget about UPSC but it was hard for him to leave the job as he was not sure about mains so he tried to do both but was not able to concentrate enough on it and he failed to reach cutoff marks

Now his hopes and dreams all went away and he decided not to go ahead with this but his family was extremely worried about him as they knew it was his dream to become IAS officer but now how can anyone change the destiny After two months he got married to his classmate to whom he had promised to marry immediately after clearing UPSC but as now latter was not possible for him so he decided to get married to her.

Again the life went back to routine and now he had totally different life and ambitions to achieve but deep down it was still hard for him to digest the situation , however his wife forced him to apply for state PSC and with his efforts he was able clear it along with his ongoing job Now he had secure government job and all things return to normal

One day his wife asked him "I know you are still interested in Civil services then why you are not giving it one more chance" Manoj remained quite as same question was harassing him daily even after securing job he was not happy as his dream was still not letting him enjoy the moment , that memories used to still haunt him but on another side he also wanted to chase it.

Again the application process for UPSC exams started , his wife insisted him to fill it up but he said that he won't get enough time to study and again it will traumatize him but at last his wife convinced him and he began the preparation as not just his wife but his mother and all relatives used to keep him boosted up , Once again that passion and urge to achieve success at any cost kept him motivated.

After clearing prelims he started studying really hard as it was do or die situation for him He used to carry notes all time with him as whenever and wherever he gets time he kept on revising it even during lunchtime he used to study as he knew every second was precious Then the mains exam went well and he was pretty much confident about clearing it Finally he got selected for Interview but this time he didn't relaxed and kept on revising as he knew he was one step away from fulfilling his dream for which he was living.

Every single second he just had one thing in mind "to study" now once again that dreams of him entering the academy where all IAS OFFICERS are trained started reappearing and finally the day of interview arrived and with god's grace all things went well Now he was eagerly waiting for the results and when results were out his all hard work was paid off as he secured AIR 13 and finally he was living his dream not only that but he became star especially for thousands of aspirants like him but the biggest moment of his life came when he finally stepped into Lal Bahadur Shastri National Academy of Administration with tears in his eyes.

31. Sharing Love

"How did you met grandma?" I asked my grandfather who was sitting next to me on the cliff of the hill as we came out for a day picnic he smiled looking at grandma ask her to tell but she asked why don't you tell the entire story and he started....back in time when I was young and used to play cricket and sometimes I used to break glass but one day I broke the glass and what I saw was a beautiful girl standing next to it I can't stop starring at her.

With few exchange of smiles we started loving each other and used to write letters and with passing time our love for eachother also grew and see it continues still today Its too hard to find such love in today's time but my grandparents are perfect example of love

One year later we are again at the same place but all of us are crying because my grandfather and grandmother has passed away although we are feeling sad but I know where ever they would be they will be sharing same love

32. "Love you, too"

"You are the only one I love." He sweetly said while he caresses my cheeks. His smile, it's luring.

"I love you too." I replied. I can already feel butterflies that flutters in my tummy.

"If I had to choose between you and another woman, I'd still choose you. I'll always choose you over anything else. You're my sunshine that lights up the dark world. You give colors to my boring life. I can't imagine my life without you, my love." He said, then a soft, romantic music played.

I am so happy. It was just my dream before, and now, the man I love the most is saying these words to me.

I smiled as he kisses my forehead. He then knelt to the ground and pulled out a small box.

I feel so nervous, yet happy because this is one of my happiest moments in life.

"Will you marry me, Scarlet?" He said as he opens the box. There is a shiny diamond ring, it's really beautiful.

"Yes! Of course! I will!" I gladly replied.

He put the ring on my finger, then he stood up and hugged me.

I hugged him back and cried.

"I love you." I whispered as I see the curtain closes.

How I wish it was real. How I wish he also loves me the way I love him. How I wish he feels the same.

We're actors, and this is just a theater play. It wasn't true. He doesn't love me too.

33. Give a rose

Give a rose to a lil inoccent child playing at the park, smilling so sweetly. Yet, later does she know a crime happened to where she stood.

Give a rose, to an old lady near the alley where a car accident happened that killed a young girl.

Give a rose, to an old couple. who had withstand many problems but love kept them together.

Give a rose, to your friends, who were ever so supportive of us and never left you when you were lost.

Give a rose, to my friends. Who supported us too and made me smile whenever we fight.

Give a rose, to your family guided you and supported you fully. As gratitude for what you had become.

Give a rose, to my family for all of their sacrifices and pain I've caused.

once their all given, smile for you have done me a favor, probably the last.

Once your done, visit me where my body lie under the ground. tell me what were their reactions, when they received a rose.

Once you're done look up at the sky. If it is sunny, I'm fine and you'll be too. if its cloudy,Cheer up that's just me admiring the clouds. If it is raining, remember to take shelter. For that is me missing you and bidding may last farewell to the earth and to you my everything..

And when you're done with everything I've requested. go back to the room we've shared. where our love lasted and where i took my last breath.

Sorry the rose is not new, that rose was the rose you gave me when we first met. now i'm giving it back to you. Smile for me my love.

34. Money

"Money can't buy happiness" - Is it so far convincing in this era......?

The word "Money" by hearing this word everyone mind blows off with jubilant. In the past times it was said that Money can't buy happiness , but current scenario has totally altered this thought. In today's era money is the only which can buy you happiness. Every step you take , you need money , and without this sweet nobody will ask who you are. Money is one of the most fundamental thing throughout everyday of life. On the off chance that we have cash, we can carry on with our life cheerfully. We can satisfy the greater part of our wants or dreams very easily. It is usually said that, "Money can't buy Happiness." It's actual in one sense, however in other sense, we can purchase or get joy through money only. On the off chance that you have money or you are rich, help somebody who is out of luck. By helping other people you get a significant serenity and genuine satisfaction in obvious sense. Feel it. Nowadays , money has become an essential part of life , if we want to live in today's era and want to show yourself towards the world , money is the only source of it. Money can give you so many things which others can't , for instance, it can give you time, it can give you superior education , it can give you luxurious lifestyle , it can give you luxurious cars and houses and many more.

The current scenario is such a like that if you are dreaming for something vast but if you are not financially sound , there is no such value of dreams, you can chase your dreams only if you have money in your hand. We can guarantee that money controls the world. Miserable yet obvious. Everything , every deed happens in this world just for the sake of this money. Why we humans are running in this life ; just for the sake this sweet i.e money because we want to feed ourselves and our family and to feed ourselves and our family , we need money to get the food. It is said that we can't live with food , but actually the scenario is like that we need money to live , if we had enough wealth , the food will automatically came to us. If we want someone to complete our task , we will offer them money , if they are satisfied with that money ,then and then only they will work for us. No matter how close you are with that person…. "No money , No honey". In the pas times, money doesn't matters in relationship , but in today's world , relationships are totally based on money. If you are wealthy healthy then everyone will come to you to keep relation with you, but once if something has happened and you are not left with that hefty amount of money, bet me people ….they will not think for once that who you are and you will just become stranger for them and here is the point where relationships are broke , no matter what kind of relation you have with that person. If you have money , keep the relation , otherwise I am on my way and you are on your way! And one thing is also final that they will also not regret for that.

On the off chance that you investigate what we as a whole accomplish for money . We go to work, the vast majority get up promptly toward the beginning of the day or keep awake until late around evening time, invest negligible time with family and need to grin in the supervisor's face just for that cheque toward the month's end. At that point, contingent upon how much your cheque is, you get the chance to do whatever it is you needed. Everything in this world happens with the give and take of money, just show some good amount of money and people will be mad upon you and they will complete each and every deed you want them to be completed. And the ironical thing is that , education is also paid in today's era , if you want to take good education , want to take admissions in high class college , just pay hefty amount of money and the admission is yours. No matter if you have pre-eminent skills or not , money will give you admissions.

But one thing is there , that with this money "With cash you can purchase a house yet not a home; With cash you can purchase a bed yet not rest; With cash you can purchase a bed yet not rest; With cash you can purchase a book yet not information; With cash you can purchase a medical clinic however not wellbeing; With cash you can purchase a position yet not regard; With cash you can purchase blood however not life; With cash you can purchase joy yet not love." If we go through the survey's , today's world is reluctantly quarrelling for money. Money makes you self-subordinate which implies that you are not any more subject to anybody yet can satisfy your life's wants all alone. With the assistance of money , you can purchase anything you like and need not approach others for it. So you can say that money enables you to act naturally reliant and there is no better inclination that this. Money gives you power which implies that you are allowed to settle on your decisions and take the choices which are best for you. One need not rely upon anybody or feel any weight as it is your life and you reserve the privilege to would what you like to. In this way you can take choices effectively regardless of what the circumstance is. But in this world everything has two sides that is "Superior & Inferior". If the almighty has given you such good amount of wealth, use it for good purpose.

In the event that you have money you can help other people you need it. There are commonly when your companions and family members would experience an emergency and may require your money related assistance. For this situation, you can without much of a stretch loan cash and help them to battle the troublesome occasions. You can offer cash to a magnanimous trust too where your cash is utilized in the correct manner to support others. Despite the fact that it is totally your decision and choice to give cash however on the off chance that you have, one can generally help other people. So from all the above things we can say that it is the "Money persecution" era and we are surviving in this era where everything starts and end with this sweet that is MONEY

.

"Money isn't everything , but everything needs money. Money will not bring you happiness, but I would rather cry in Mercedes than in a bus."

35. Party Phobia

"The decoration was done and all plan for party was going well now just I have to remind the caterers but the Jack was really possessed about party and he was repeatedly looking at checklist even after I assured him that everything is going according to plan

Now finally the party evening started and our friends also arrived but we were still in that clothes so we hurried towards the dressing room and changed the clothes after trying and testing several hairstyles we finally got ready and till time we came out every one was there so I asked DJ to play the music and with that everyone started dancing with lots of hustle bustle and loud noises we all became deaf and just got in our own zones

After half an hour I got call from Jack but due to loud music I was not able to hear anything so searched him but he was nowhere I came outside and try to call him but he didn't answered sometime later I received his call he said to manage the party for few minutes as he will back in sometime and before listening to me he ended the call and after few minutes we heard the extremely loud noise as if something huge had fallen and we ran outwards ...."

"Sir is calling you"

Ok wait what u said until now has been recorded the police stopped me and asked me to wait outside for sometime

"We were going to take admission in same medical college and we had planned about so many things in future and then suddenly he took this step.... For two years we had really worked very hard and when it was the time for us to celebrate he left me alone..." The police interrupted me and asked does anything suspicious you noticed in his behaviour from few days but there was nothing like that then why one would take such extreme step that question was really eating me out

He achieved what he wanted but what about achievement when he himself is not there what to do now why he took such step? His parents were not ready to accept the reality just like us but we can't change it now.In order to achieve something in life we make ourselves so isolated that sometimes even we can't hear our own voices, But what's the use of such enchanting when we have already in loss.

Days passed away everyone got back in their life, police also closed the investigation. I was in my college starting new journey of my life but still the thought of being alone here was pinching my heart and then announcement was made for Freshers party and just the word "party" was enough to bring all those memories back and to such extent that after that day I had actually developed phobia for parties and I had tried hard to overcome it but even after three decades it's futile.

36. Wallpaper

We bought an old house, . My father is in charge of the "new" construction – converting the kitchen in to the master bedroom for instance, while I'm on wallpaper removal duty. The previous owner papered EVERY wall and CEILING! Removing it is brutal, but oddly satisfying. The best feeling is getting a long peel, similar to your skin when you're peeling from a sunburn. I don't know about you but I make a game of peeling, on the hunt for the longest piece before it rips.Under a corner section of paper in every room is a person's name and a date. Curiosity got the best of me one night when I Googled one of the names and discovered the person was actually a missing person, the missing date matching the date under the wallpaper! The next day, I made a list of all the names and dates. Sure enough each name was for a missing person with dates to match. We notified the police who naturally sent out the crime scene team. They were completely clueless about the the scene but with further investigation they found that the owner of the house gave the house to a person who was drug dealer and also involved in kidnapping , finally he got arrested but it's still a mystery that how that names came under that wallpaper

37. Last Day

A father who had just one day left to retire from the 35 years job whom he loved the most

A son who had just two days to go for the completion of his college after 4 years of studies

A daughter who had to just three days left before she leave her parents house and settle down in all new country with her in laws permanently

And then comes the mother who had nothing special but have to live the life in all new way as all her closed are about to end the beautiful parts of their life and going to start a new journey

Everyone had their all pains and emotions of leaving behind the things and for each of them the memories were different but only mother was there to understand the feeling of all but everyone has to say only one thing " you can't understand my feelings because you are not at my place"

But how can someone explain to them that she was the person who can feel the most as she was part of everyone journeys and she had actually seen all of them growing in their own path

38. That White Poison

It was my pediatric exam and we all were allotted the patients and we have to take detailed history of the patient. I was alloted the 9 year old boy Raja he seems to be cooperative as he responded to my basic questions well

He was very much curious to know about the process I asked about his family history as it was part of my questionnaire he replied that he lives with his mother and his sister as his father died a year ago as I further inquired he told that his father died because of white poison which he was addicted to I asked him more so he said that white poison (basically tobacco snuff) caused him mouth cancer and he died of that.

He further told me that most of his friends are also addicted to it and he constantly ask them to stop that as he doesn't want anyone else to go through same miseries that his family went through when his father was diagnosed with oral cancer

39. Travelogue

We woke up early in the morning had our breakfast and resumed our journey from Champaranya, Chhattisgarh now we were heading to the Orissa Again we have to spend entire day travelling in bus we took just one halt for lunch and then continued I was amazed to see how the lifestyle and cultures were changing as we were travelling from one state to another finally we reached the Jagannath Puri ,Orissa after 15 hrs of journey we straight went to our hotel, Nilachal bhakti Niwas as we were tired.

It was still dark when we woke up we got freshen up and went to the Jagannath Puri temple to attend the mangla arti after standing in queue for 45 minutes , the temple is quite big and there's a iron pillar in front of the gate there are lots of stories associated with it after that we went back to hotel had breakfast and took some rest, as it was planned after lunch we went to see the largest sun temple of India konark around 30 km from Puri the entire temple is inscribed with the small shrines of God and goddesses in various positions it is well known for its artform as lots of foreigners visits these place daily after that we went to see Chandrabhaga beach one of the cleanest beach of India which is also the hub for meditation

The Chandrabhaga beach is also famous for its sunset view and luckily we got chance to view it this place also hold mythological importance after that we returned back to our stay at Puri and had our dinner.

Once again we resumed our journey from Puri now our next destination was Bhubaneswar which took almost 2 hrs . We visited the Lingraja temple which is famous for its sculptures the huge temple is constructed in such a way that the environment inside the temple remains constant there are Sanskrit shlokas inscribed all over the temple Other than this Bhubaneswar also has caves and museum and it's the main hub for the fabric work ikat

Then after having lunch at Bhubaneswar we headed towards next stop that is Kolkata where we reach at night

Our day started with breakfast at our stay, hotel Akash, Howrah it was quite spacious and affordable hotel, then we decided to visit few nearby places as others would be covered in Kolkata darshan

Post lunch we visited the Belur Math its main headquarters of Ramakrishna mission there are museums and temples dedicated to Ramakrishna Paramhansa founded by his disciple Swami Vivekanand on the bank of river Hooghly after that we went to millennium park which is a nature park with fun rides as it was evening the atmosphere was pleasant and we were enjoying the view of Howrah and Hooghly

40. The haunted School

The bell rang and students start rushing towards the gate as everyone was in hurry to reach the home as it was winter the sky was slowly getting less brighter with clock approaching towards 6 Now the entire school was silent and gates were getting closed

After about an hour one of the Watchman heard some noise but he ignored it then again he heard the same noise so now he went towards the playground but no one was there he went towards backside of school also but no one was there so he decided to return but while returning he again heard the noise now he followed it and it was coming from ground floor washroom which was locked from outside he reached towards the door and shouted Is there anyone inside but received no response

 So he started walking back then suddenly he heard someone shouting please open the door he immediately went towards the keyroom picked up the washroom key and went straight to open the door but what he saw afterwards was really scary there was a boy sitting on the floor with arms folded and his entire body was shivering and on seeing the Watchman he pointed towards the mirror above the washbasin where it was written help in red block letters

Watchman asked the boy what happened and looking at his condition he took him out and called another guard he asked the boy how he got locked and who had written this but boy was still shivering so they closed the door and took the boy to their cabin

They gave glass of water to that boy and asked his name and his parents contact so they can inform them but boy was so scared that he was not able to speak a single word so the Watchman called the school secretary he also tried to calm the boy by telling him that he is safe now and there is nothing to worry within few minutes the secretary came to school and he also asked the details so he gave his father s number and finally his parents were called to take the child back home

Meanwhile secretary kept asking what happened and how he got locked but he didn't replied As soon as the boys parents arrived he started crying his parents were also worried and they asked the same question now he started describing the events " when the school bell rang I can downwards and then I went to washroom on the ground floor but when I was returning someone called my name so I turned back and what I saw... He gasped for a moment and then continued the help was written on the mirror I was scared but before I can move suddenly someone closed the door I ran ran towards it and asked to open the door but no one helped me " his parents asked secretary that how can someone lock the door this way to this secretary said" Sir generally the peons checks the washroom before locking them and this has happened for first time but we are extremely sorry for and I am assuring you that we will strictly look after this mistake "

The secretary called the peon but he said that he checked the washroom before locking it and no one was there and nothing was written on mirror. Now secretary was in dilemma to believe in whose story so he informed about the entire incident to the principal

The same thing happened again after few days now the another boy got locked inside the same washroom and he also heard the voice asking for help These news spread all across the town even the media got involved in it So the parents union complain about the incident to the principal and asked for immediate action Even the rumours started about the ghost in the school and it became the talk of the town

Principal immediately asked to permanently close that washroom on the ground floor and committee was made to look after the events so as to assure the parents Now the things started to normalise and nothing unusual happened for months

But one night around 11 pm when guard was roaming around the ground he heard that someone is knocking the door he went ahead and to his astonishment the voice was coming from same washroom which was closed 6 months ago he called his another colleague and both were scared and informed to the secretary who immediately came to school and still the knock was heard They informed to principal and asked for permission to open the door but when they opened the door no one was there inside and HELP was written on the mirror

After that the school was shut and till date no one dares to pass through it after evening